The Hot Cross Buns Book

for Cello

by Cassia Harvey

CHP153

©2006 by C. Harvey Publications All Rights Reserved.

www.charveypublications.com - print books
www.learnstrings.com - PDF downloadable books
www.harveystringarrangements.com - chamber music

1. Hot Cross Buns

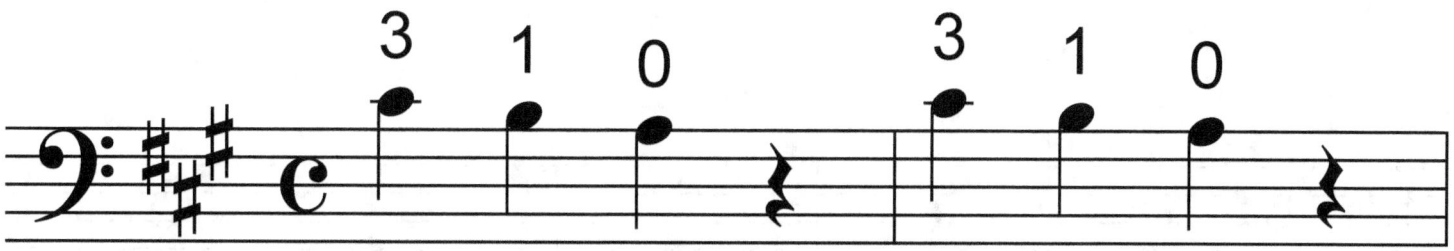

2. Hot Cross Buns with Half Notes

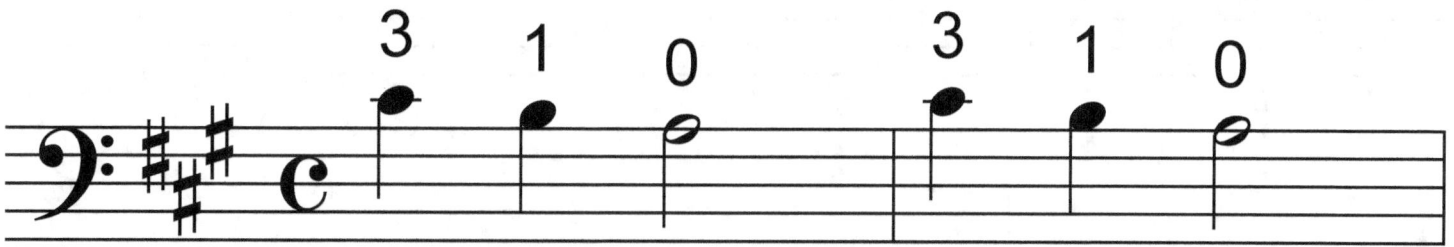

3. Hot Cross Buns with Rests

4. Hot Cross Rhythm

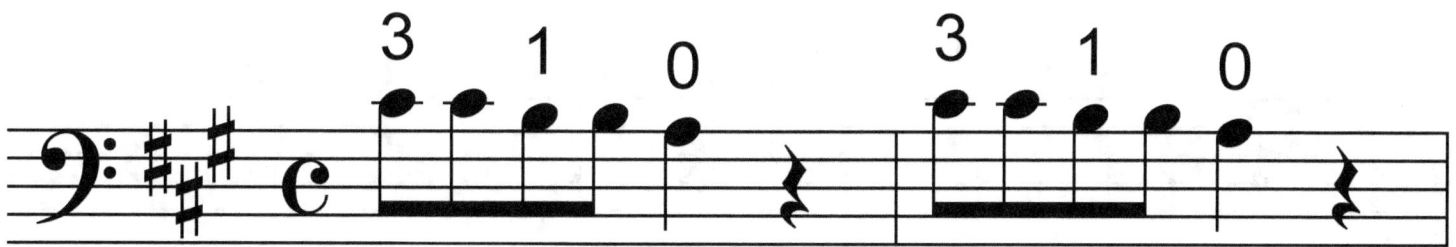

5. Hot Cross Rhythm

6. Hot Cross Buns on D

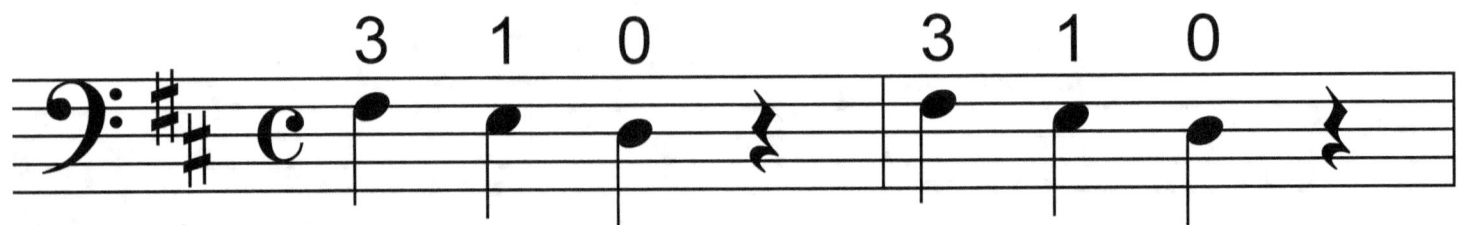

7. Hot Cross Rhythm

©2006 C. Harvey Publications All Rights Reserved.

8. Hot Cross Buns Marching

9. Hot Cross Buns Running

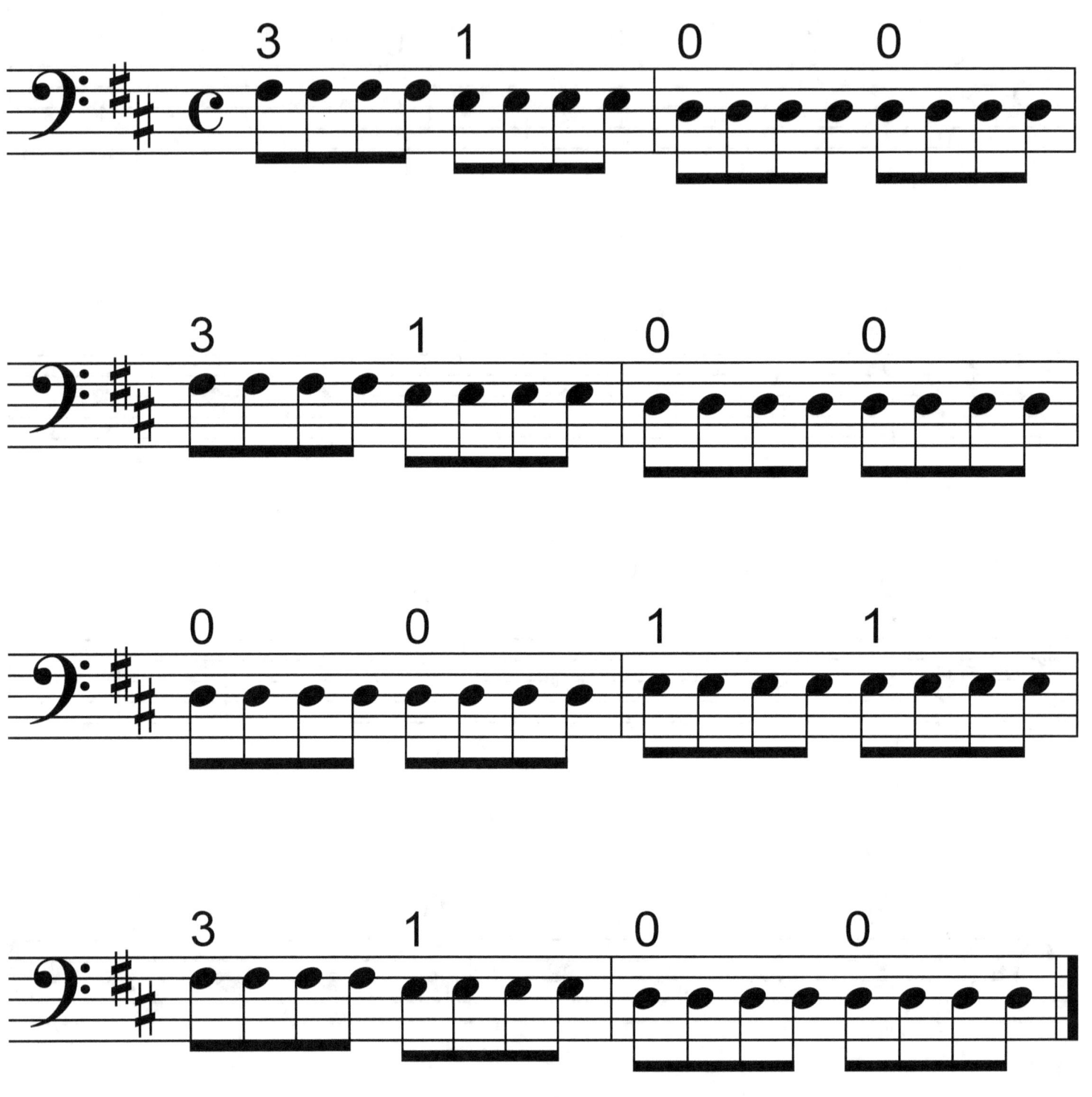

10. Hot Cross Buns on G

11. Hot Cross Buns with Half Notes

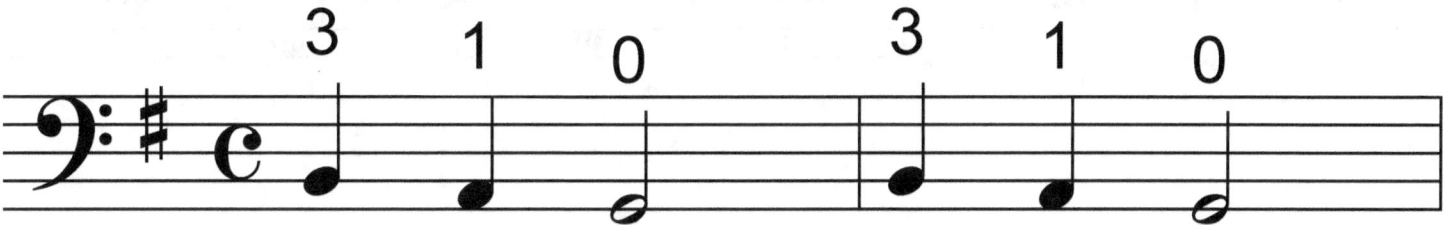

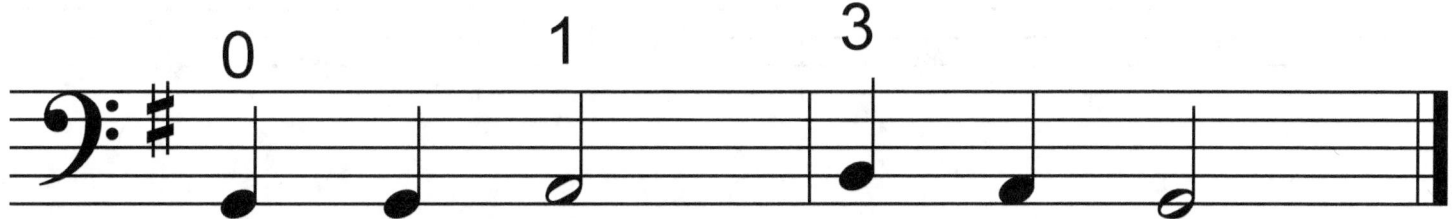

12. Hot Cross String Changing

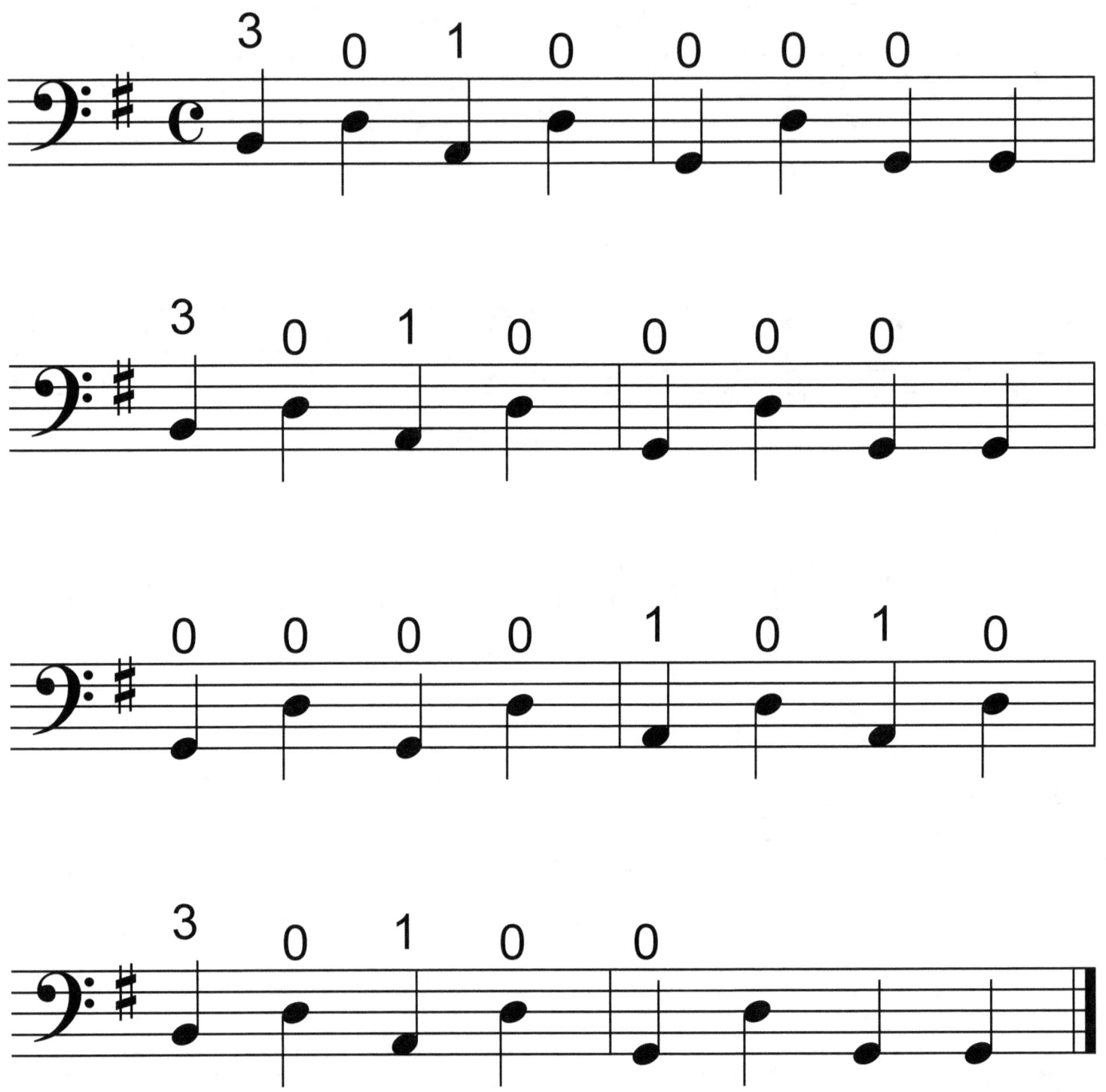

13. Hot Cross Rhythm

14. Hot Cross Buns on C

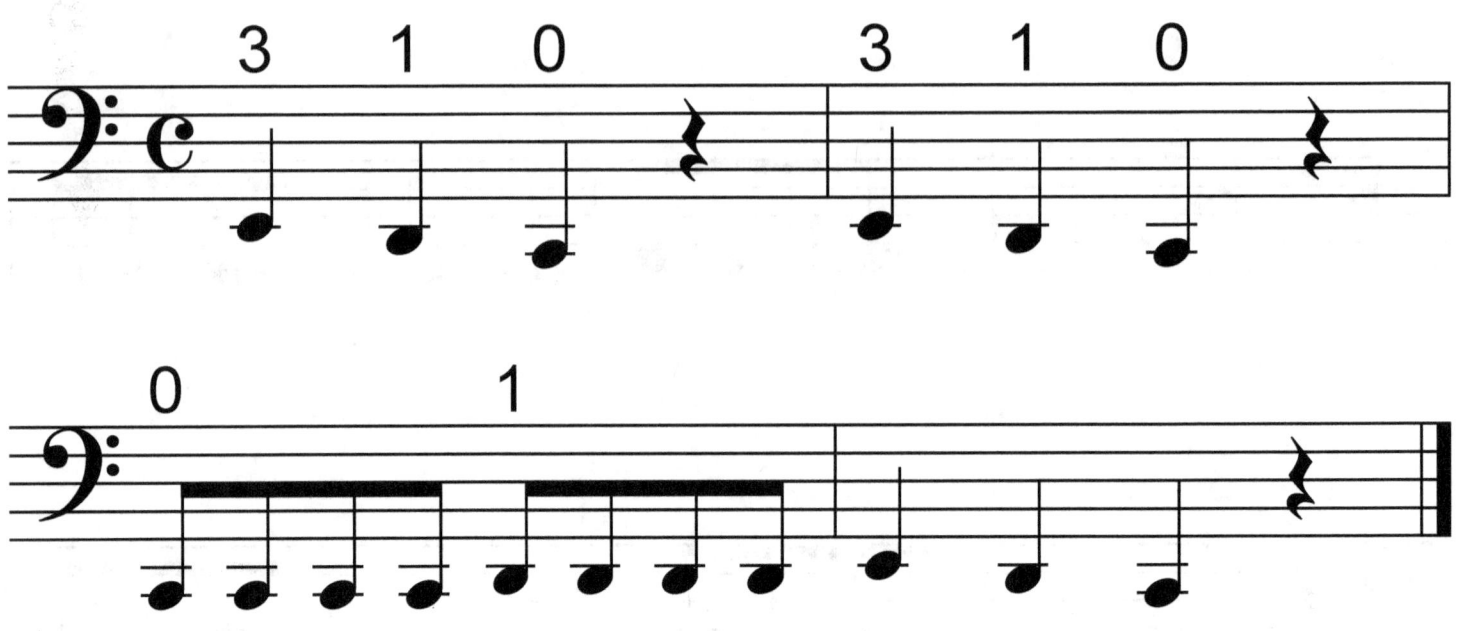

15. Hot Cross Buns with Rests

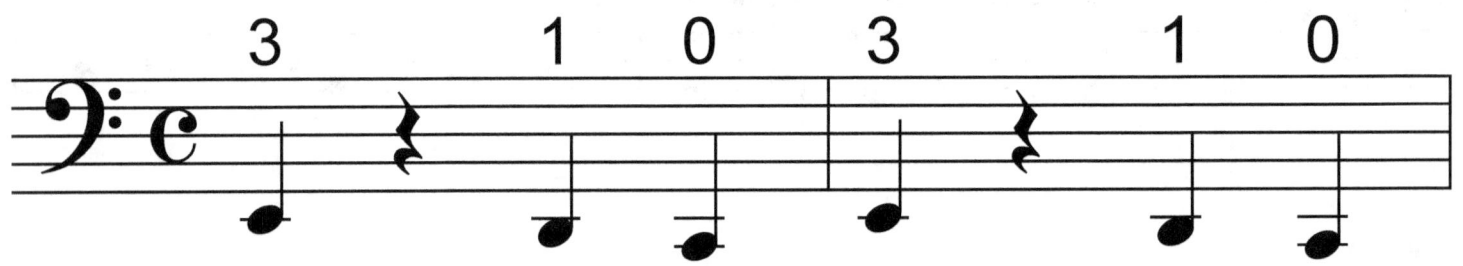

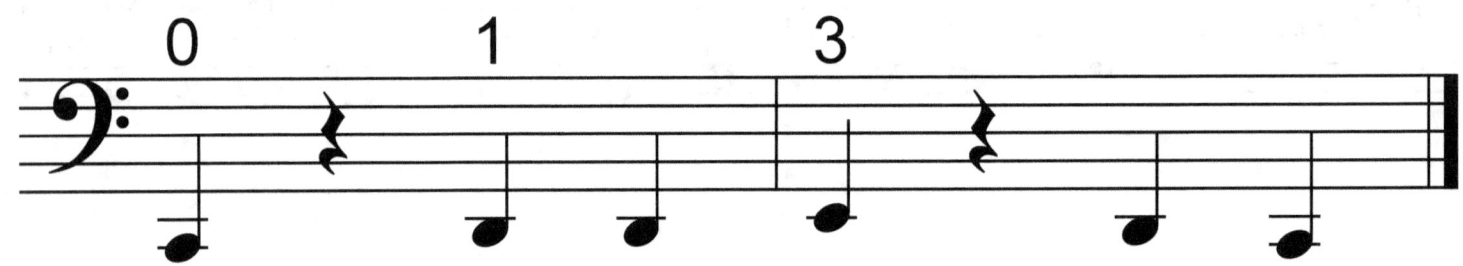

16. Hot Cross Rhythm

17. Hot Cross String Changing

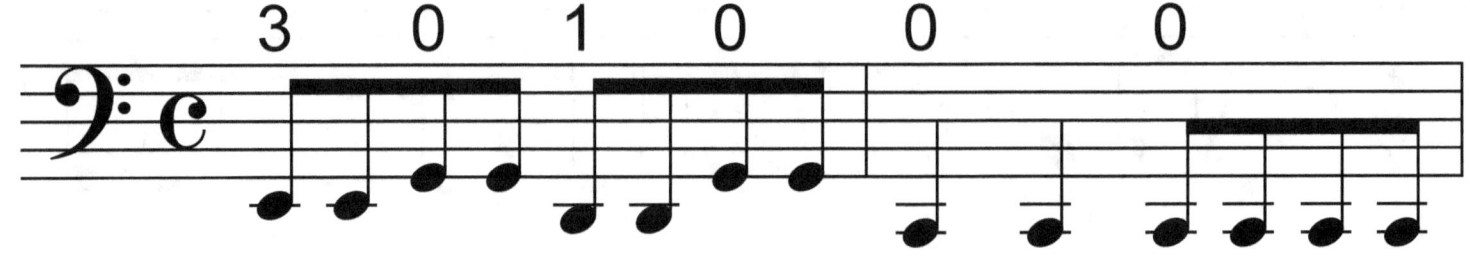
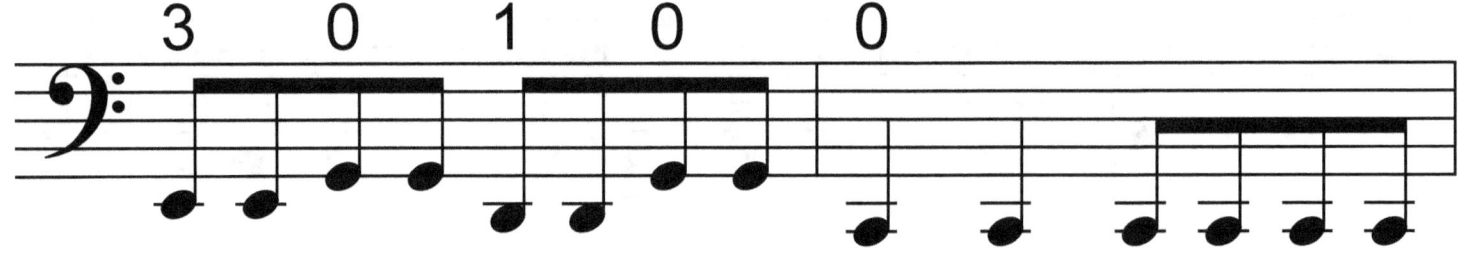
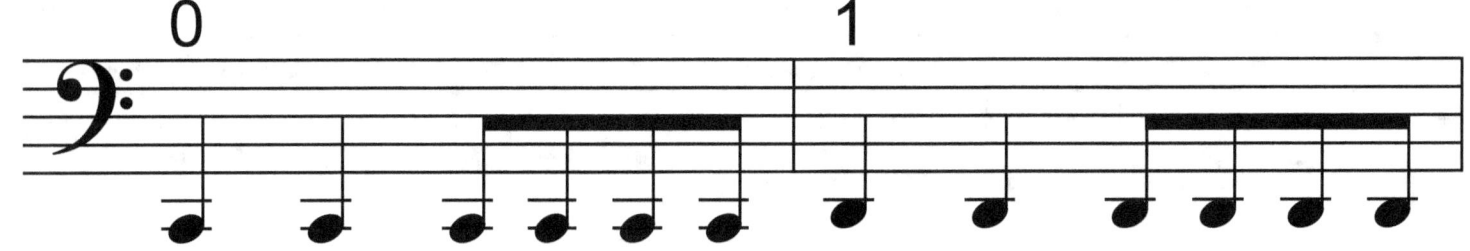
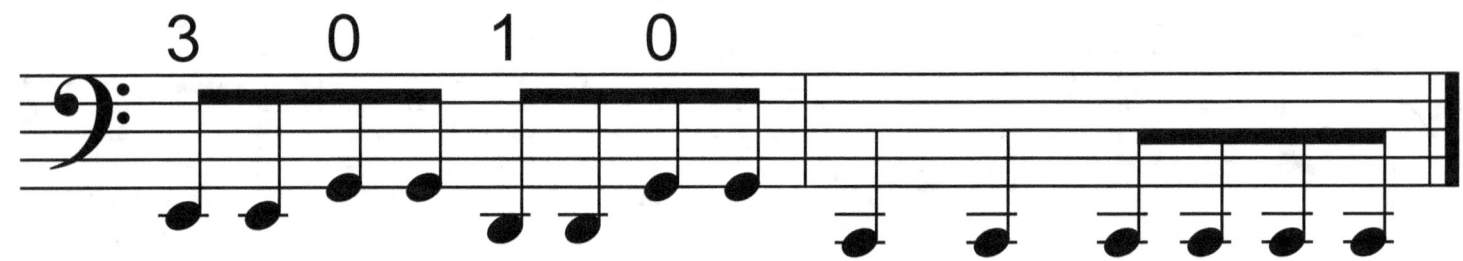

18. Cold Cross Buns

19. Cold Cross Double Stops

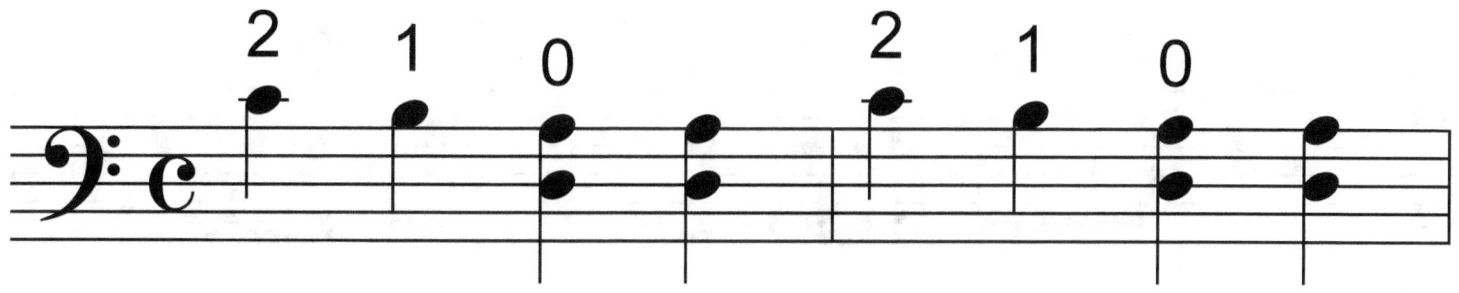
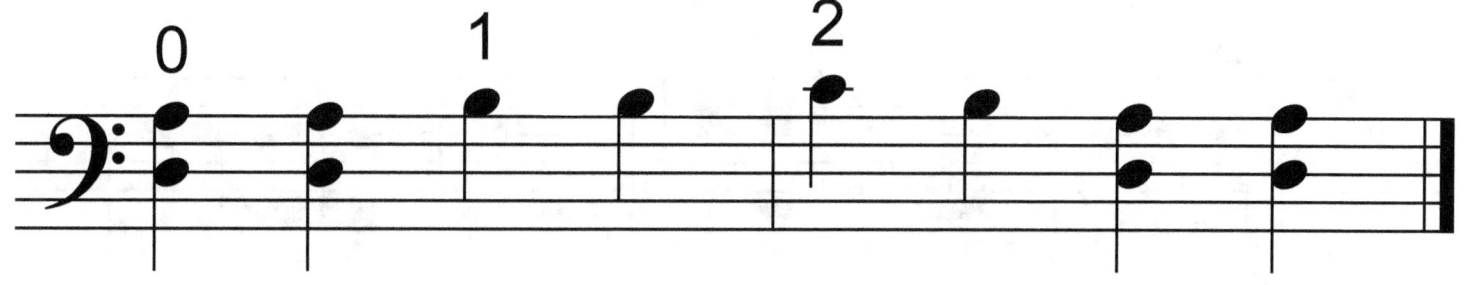

20. Cold Cross Buns on D

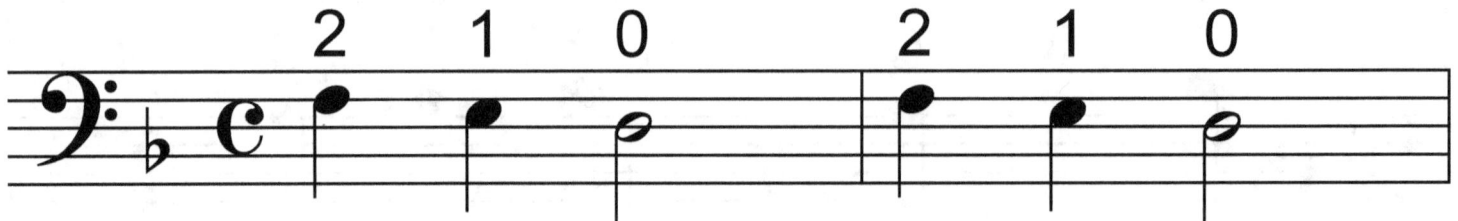

21. Cold Cross Rhythm on D

22. Cold Cross Buns on G

23. Cold Cross Double Stops

24. Cold Cross Buns on C

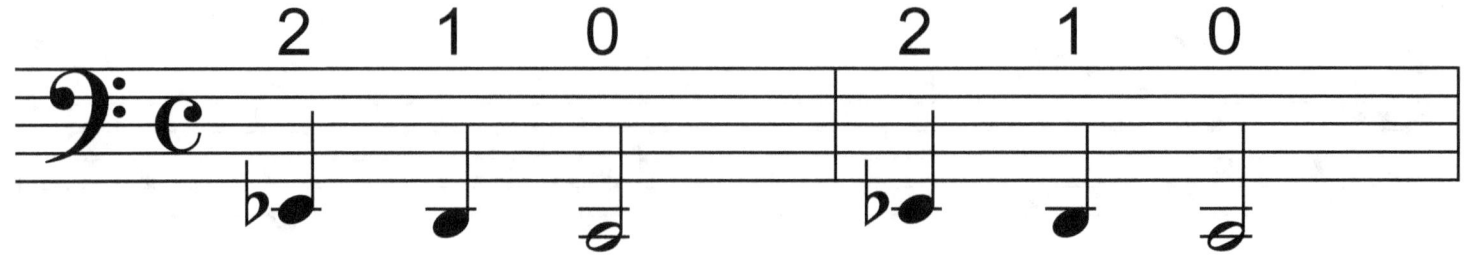

25. Cold Cross String Crossing

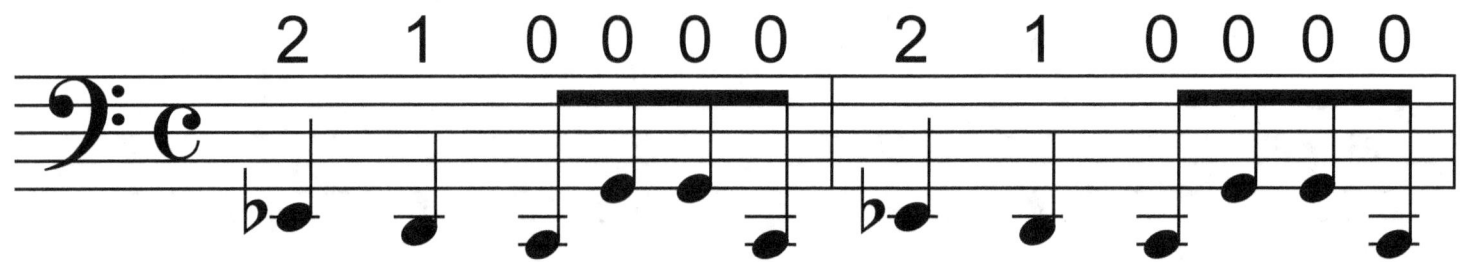

©2006 C. Harvey Publications All Rights Reserved.

26. Hot Cross Buns with Open A

27. Hot Cross Rhythm

28. Hot Cross Rhythm

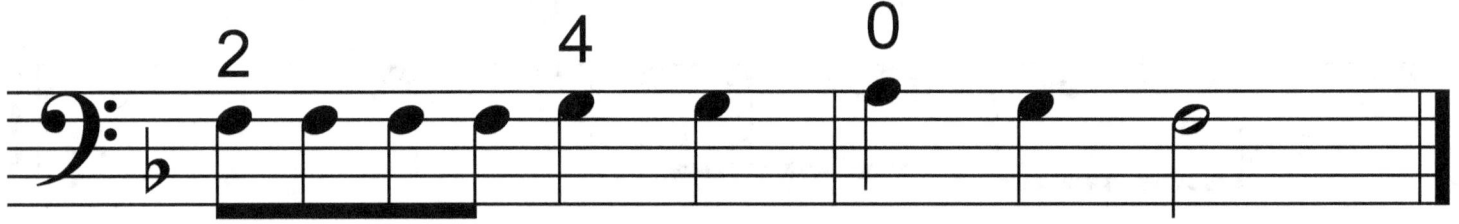

29. Hot Cross Eighth Notes

©2006 C. Harvey Publications All Rights Reserved.

30. Hot Cross Buns with Open D

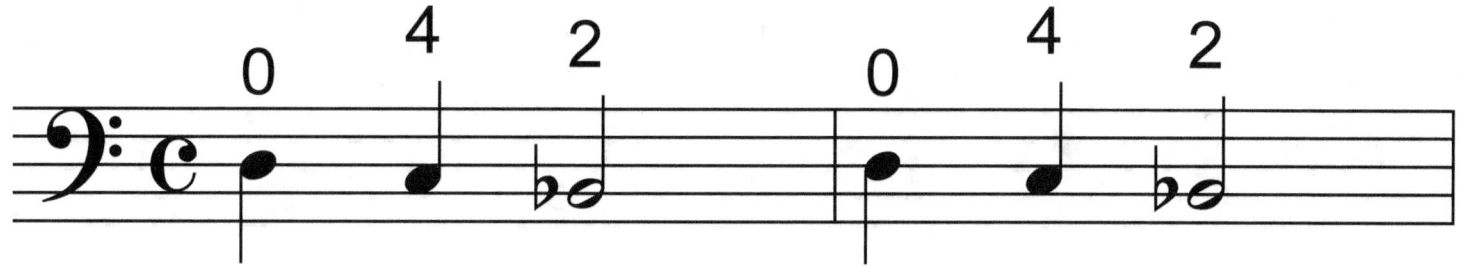

31. Hot Cross Rests and Half Notes

32. Hot Cross Variation

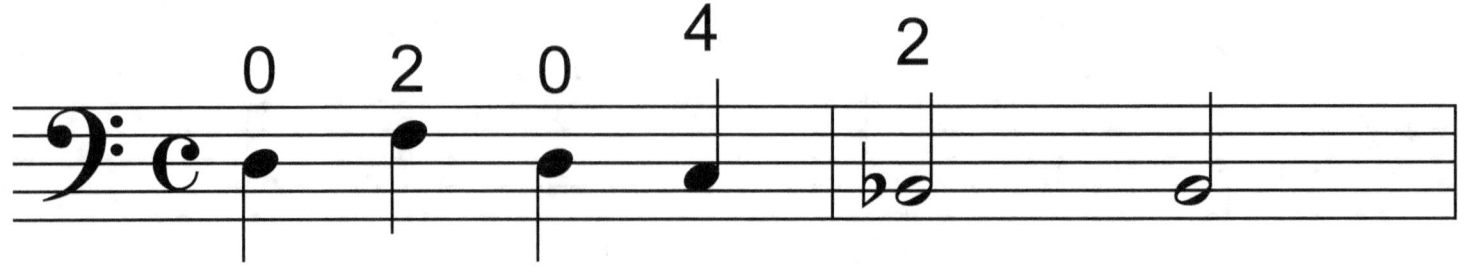

33. Hot Cross Buns with Open G

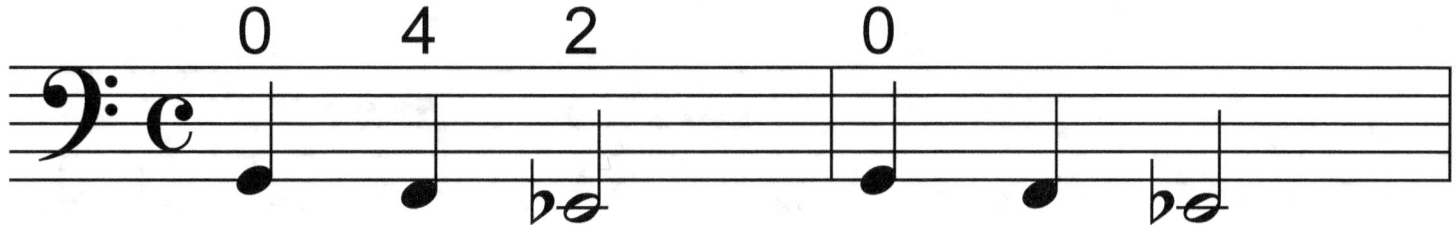

34. Hot Cross Rhythm

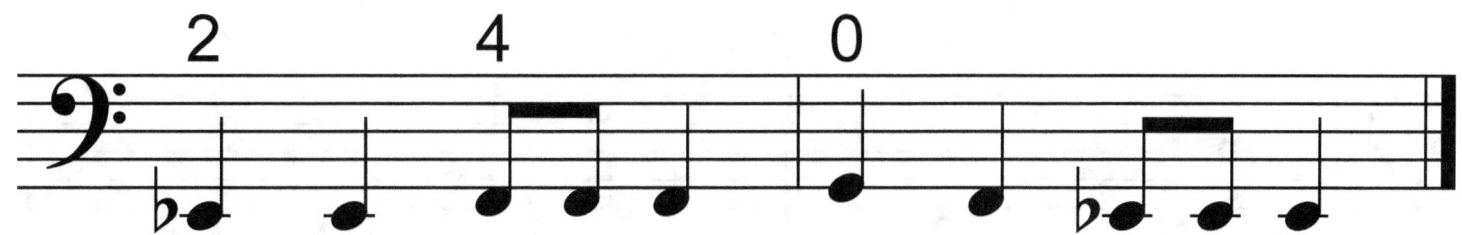

35. Hot Cross Long-Short-Short

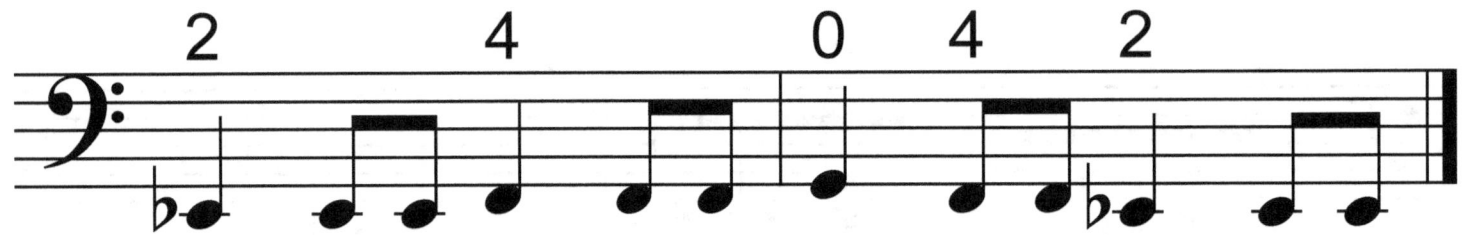

36. Hot Cross Rhythm

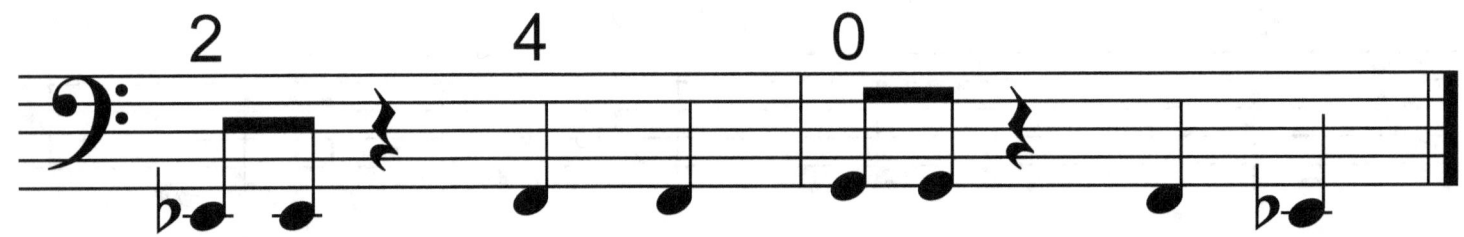

37. Hot Cross Buns with First Finger

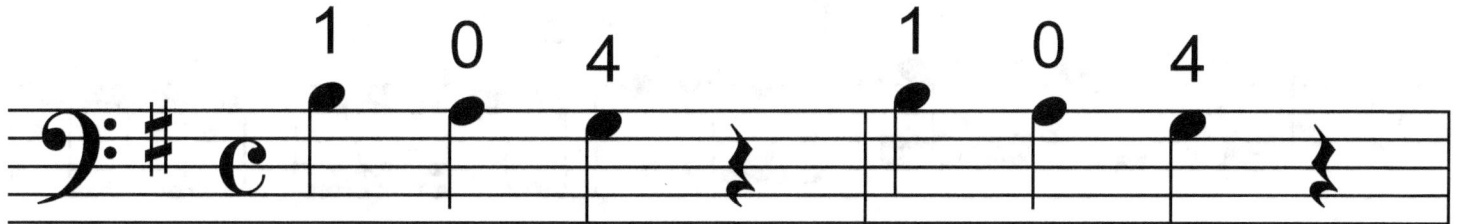

38. Hot Cross Buns String Crossing

39. Hot Cross Rhythm

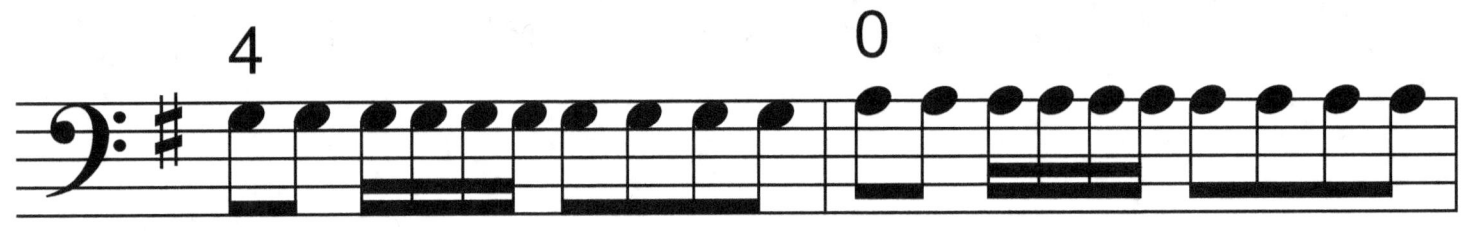
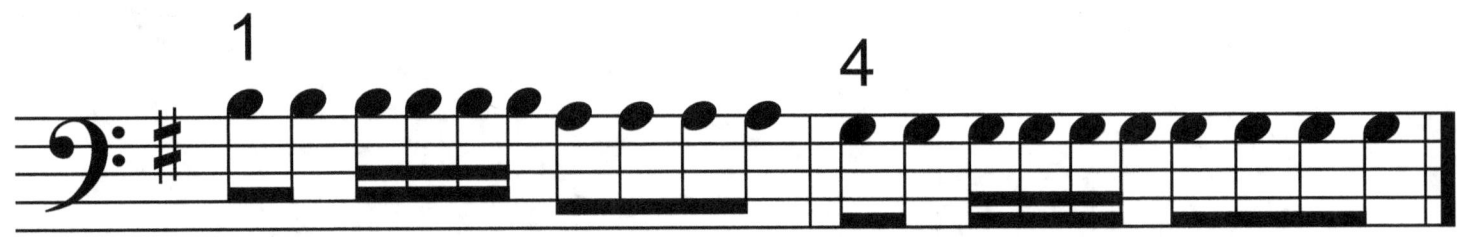

40. Hot Cross Buns with First Finger

41. Hot Cross Buns String Crossing

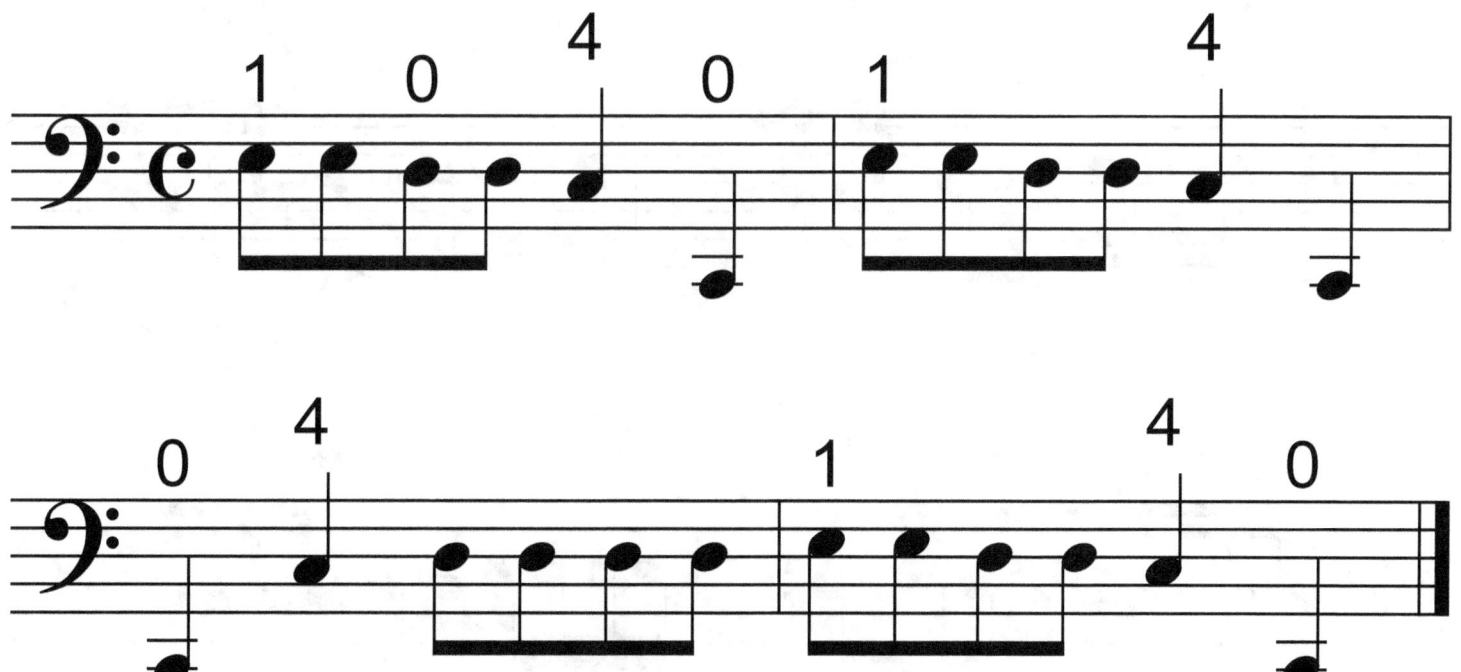

42. Hot Cross Rhythm

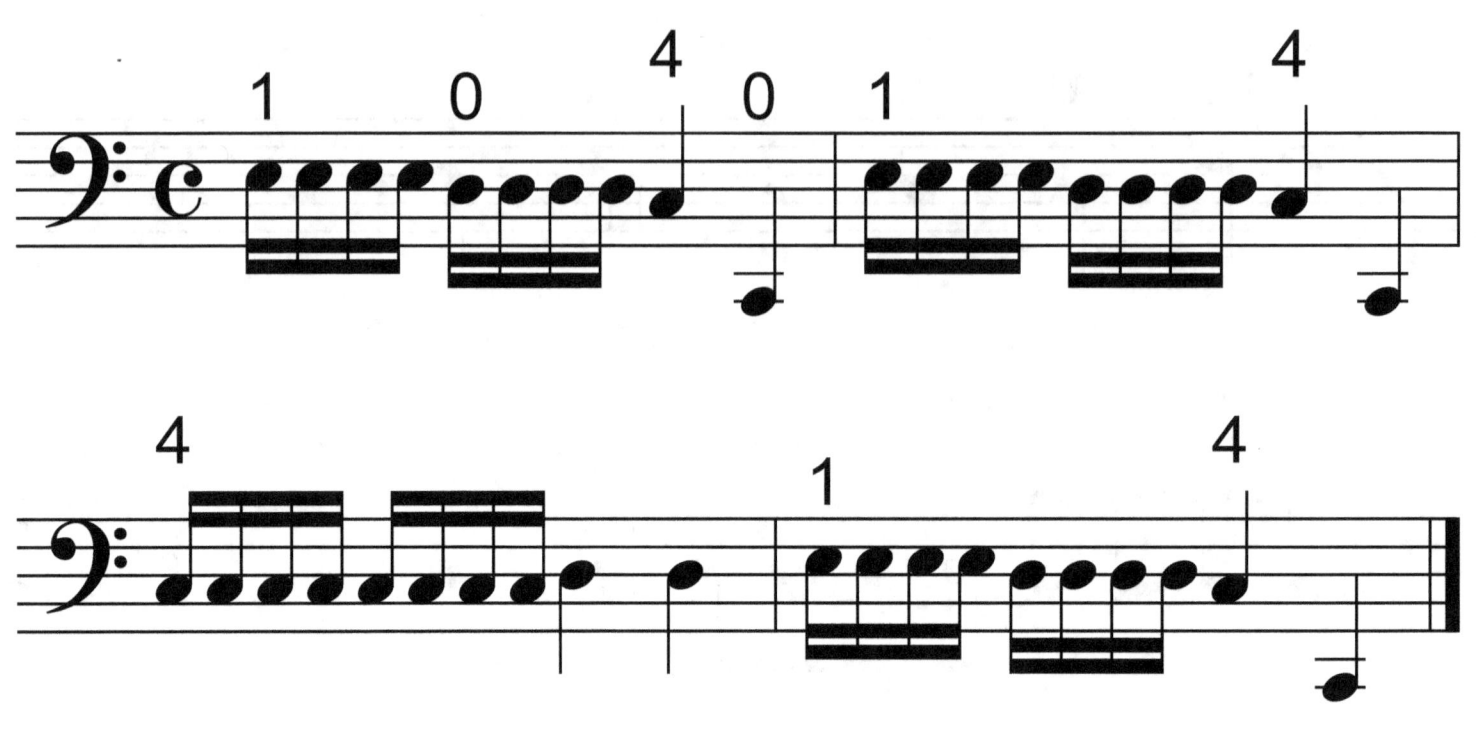

43. Hot Cross Rhythm Variation

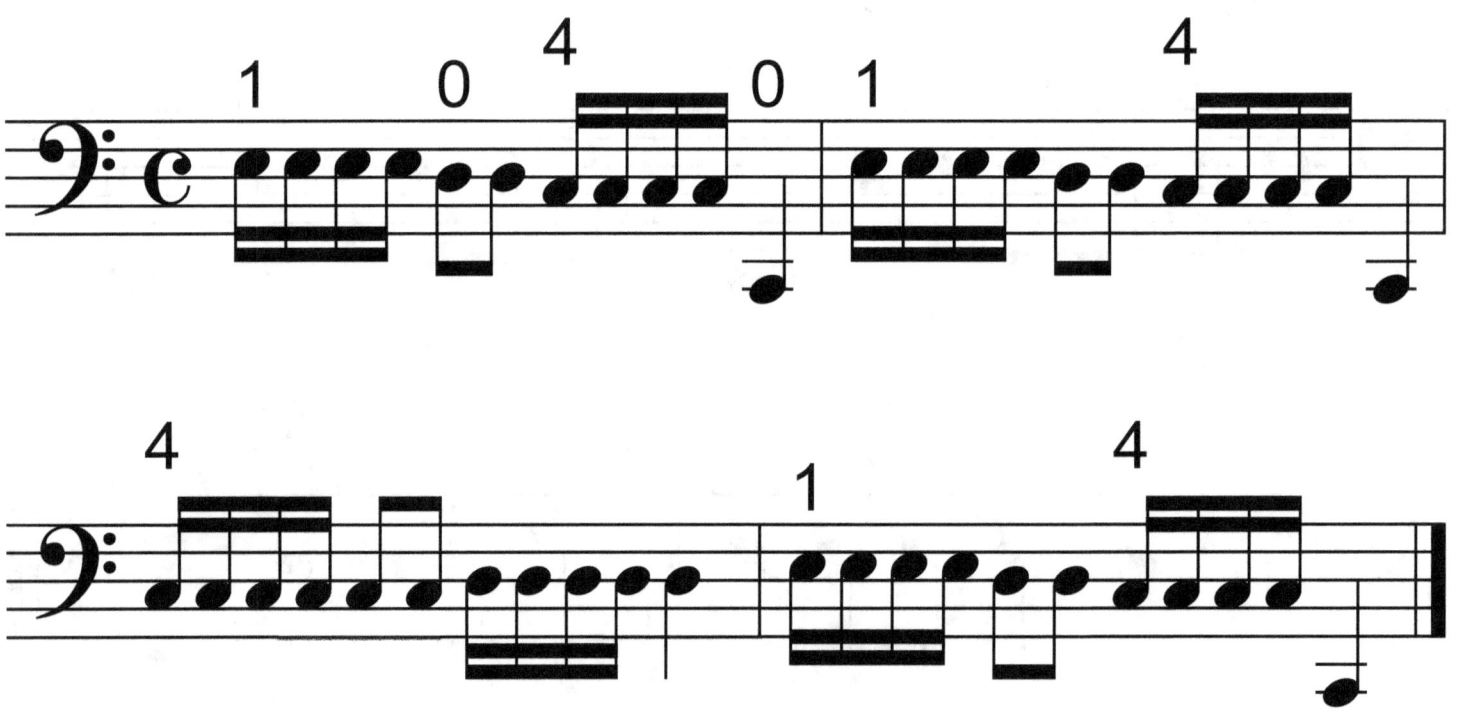

©2006 C. Harvey Publications All Rights Reserved.

44. Hot Cross Buns with First Finger

45. Hot Cross Rhythm

46. Hot Cross Octaves

47. Hot Cross Eighth Note Octaves

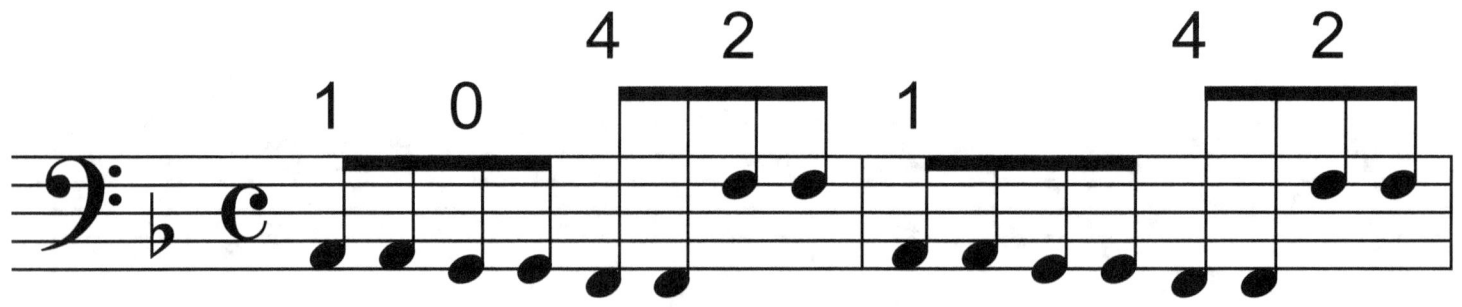
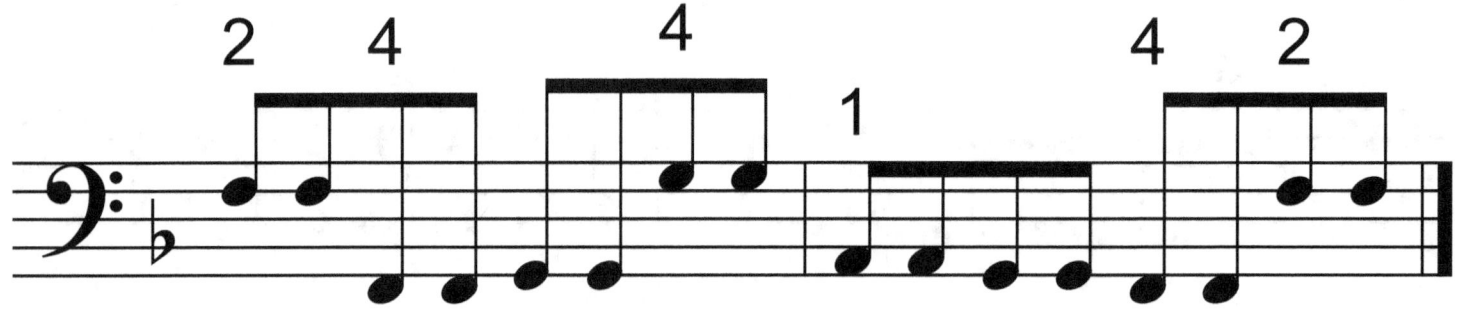

48. Hot Cross String Crossing

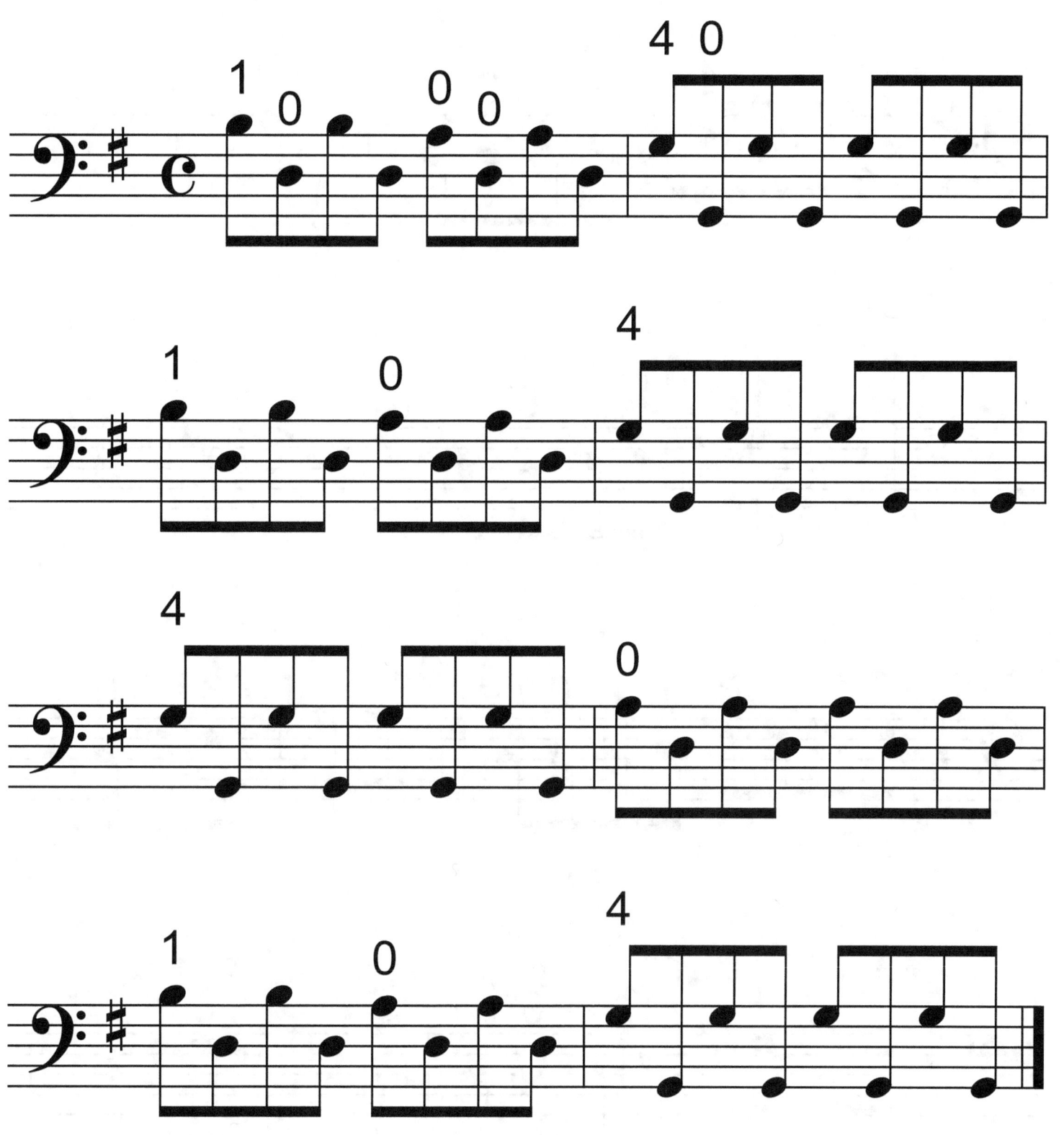

49. Hot Cross First Fiddle Tune

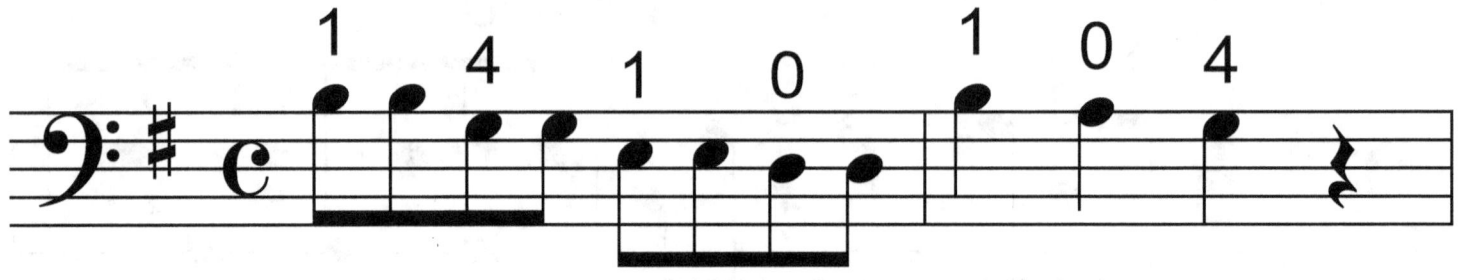
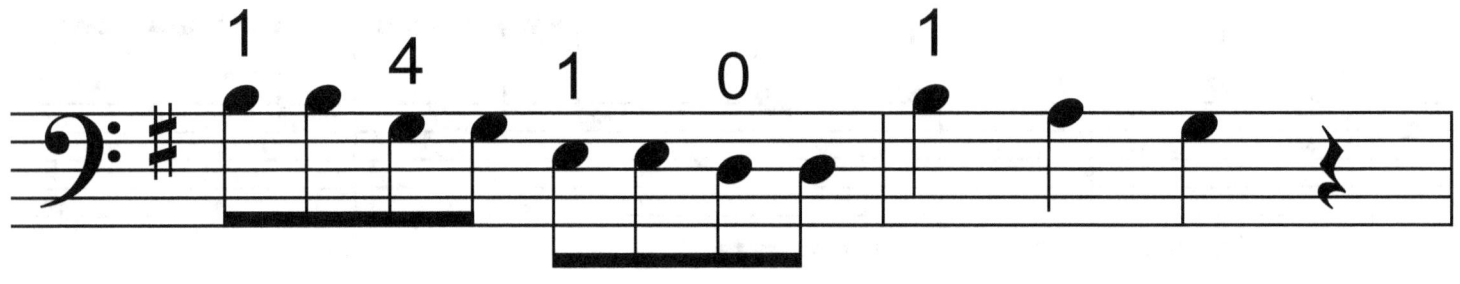
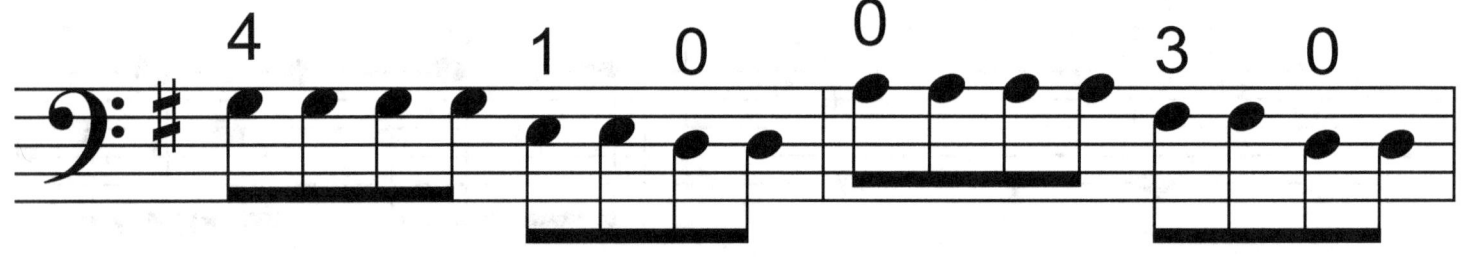
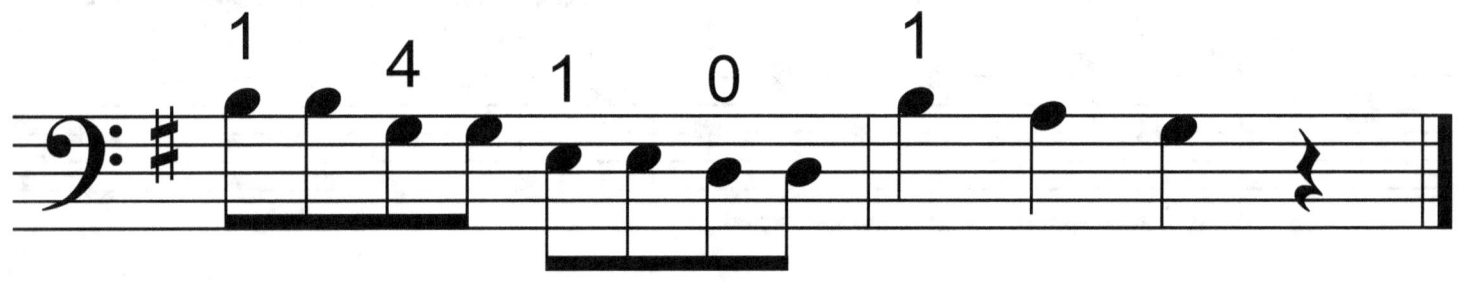

50. Hot Cross Second Fiddle Tune

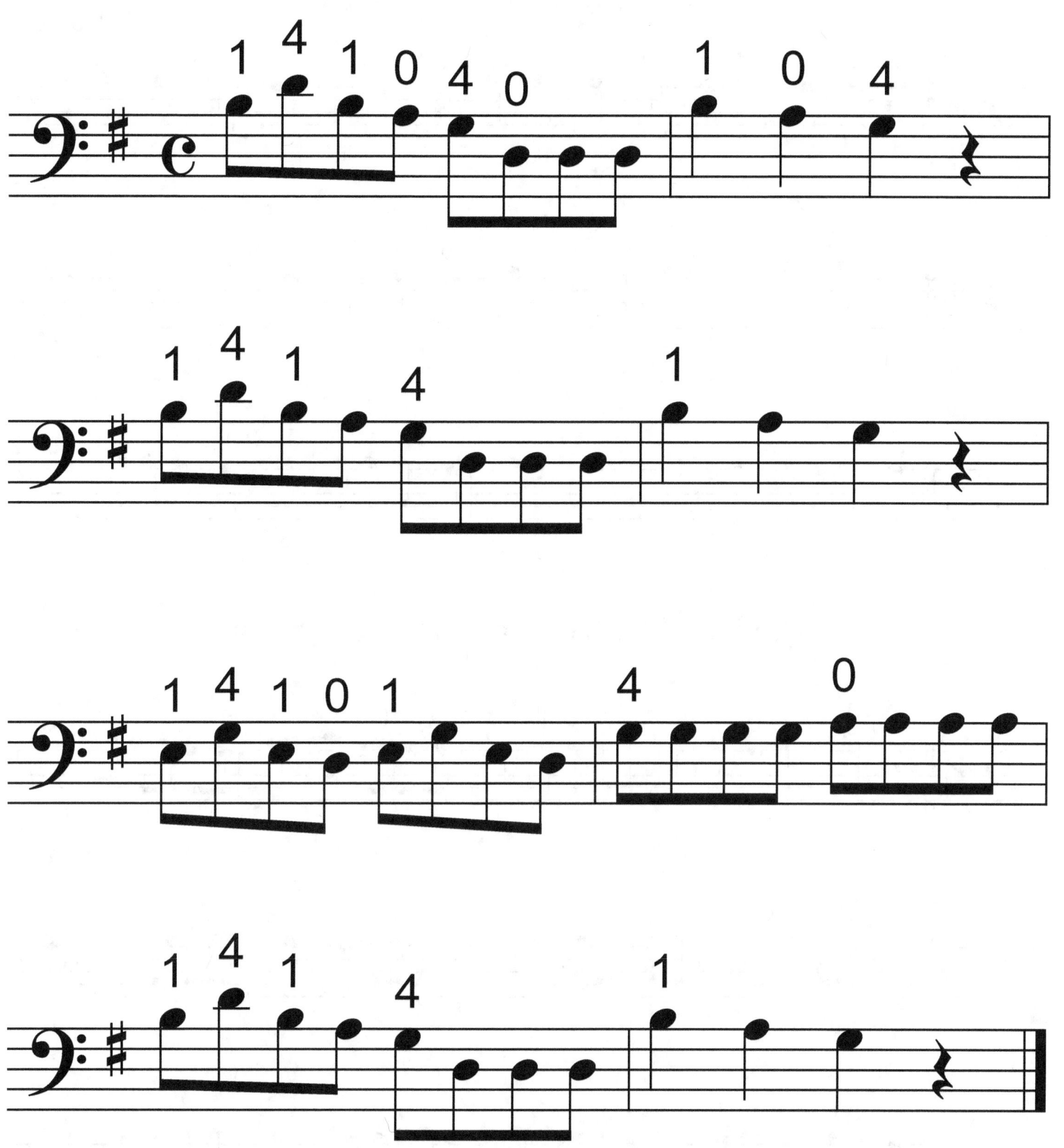

available from www.charveypublications.com: CHP221

Cello Book One

A, B, and C#

Cassia Harvey

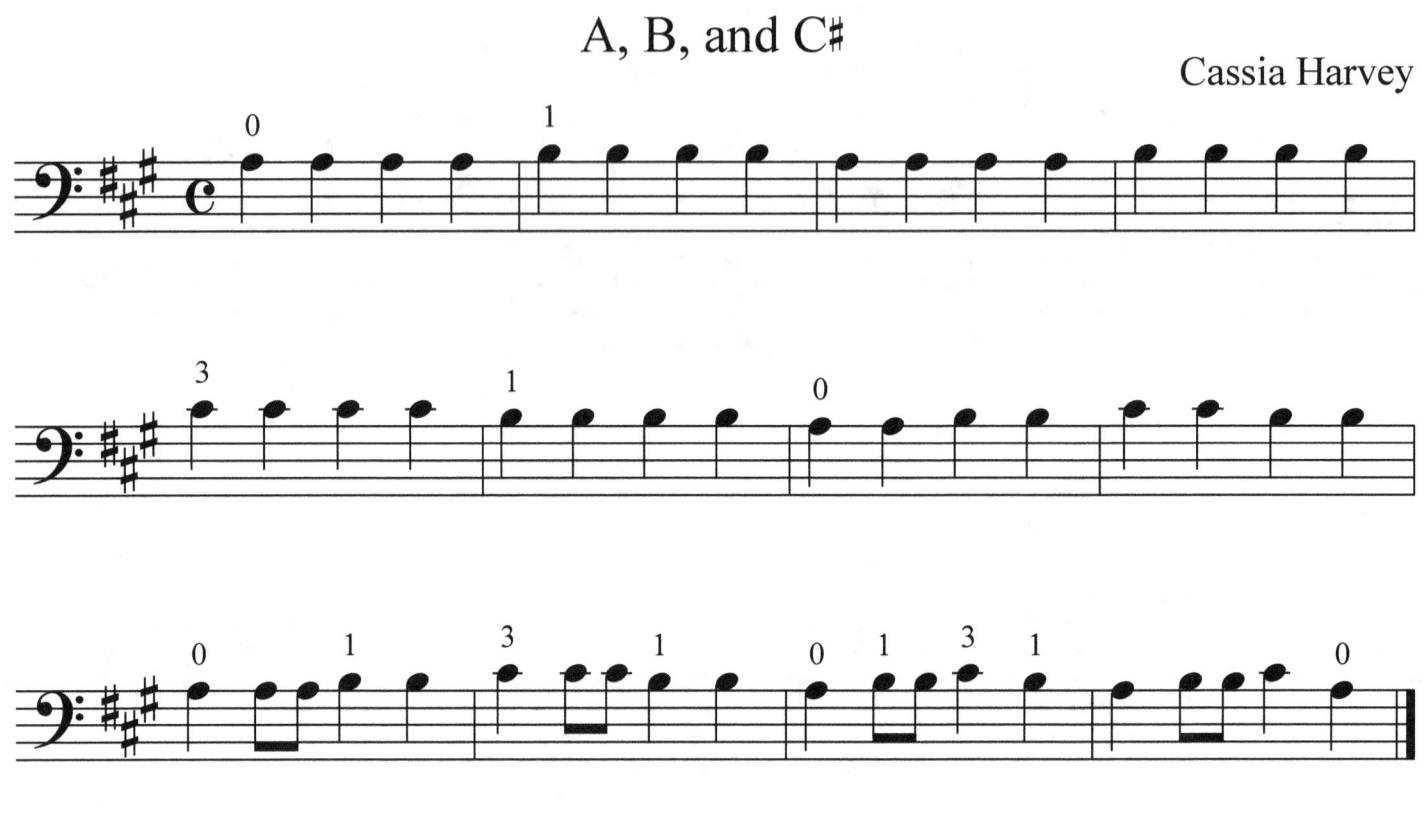

The Ladybug: A Hungarian Folk Song

©2012 C. Harvey Publications All Rights Reserved.